CRIME SOLVERS

COMPUTER EVIDENCE

by Amy Kortuem

raintree

a Capstone company — publishers for children

Raintree is an imprint of Capstone Global Library Limited, a company incorporated in England and Wales having its registered office at 264 Banbury Road, Oxford, OX2 7DY – Registered company number: 6695582

www.raintree.co.uk
myorders@raintree.co.uk

Edited by Carrie Braulick Sheely
Designed by Kayla Rossow
Original illustrations © Capstone Global Library
Picture research by Svetlana Zhurkin
Production by Kris Wilfahrt
Originated by Capstone Global Library Ltd
Printed and bound in India

ISBN 978 1 4747 7504 5 (hardback)
22 21 20 19 18
10 9 8 7 6 5 4 3 2 1

ISBN 978 1 4747 6335 6 (paperback)
23 22 21 20 19
10 9 8 7 6 5 4 3 2 1

British Library Cataloguing in Publication Data
A full catalogue record for this book is available from the British Library.

Acknowledgements
We would like to thank the following for permission to reproduce photographs: Alamy: keith morris, 19; Courtesy of the Federal Bureau of Investigation, 7, 22, 29; Getty Images: AFP/Jay Directo, 23 (top), Pool/Gary W. Green, 27; Newscom: Science Photo Library/Tek Image, 20, Zuma Press/Jebb Harris, 23 (bottom), 25; Shutterstock: Alexander Geiger, 16, Bing Wen, 28, charnsitr, 15, Eviart, 12, Farosofa, 13, Gorodenkoff, 9 (top), igorstevanovic, 21, ioat, 9 (bottom), kaprik, 14, Presslab, 18, rawf8, 5, Rawpixel, 10, Redpixel.pl, cover, 17. Design Elements by Shutterstock

CONTENTS

Chapter 1
Clues left on a computer 4

Chapter 2
Types of computer crimes 8

Chapter 3
Finding and gathering computer evidence 18

Chapter 4
Computer evidence at work 26

Glossary 30
Find out more 31
Comprehension questions 32
Index 32

Clues left on a computer

A worker opens an email and clicks on a link. A computer **virus** spreads. It shuts down all the company's computers. The company's owner calls the police.

> **virus** hidden computer program that copies itself and harms computers

Police study the email. It traces back to a computer. Clues left on the computer show a former employee of the company probably made the virus. Computer **evidence** helps to solve the crime.

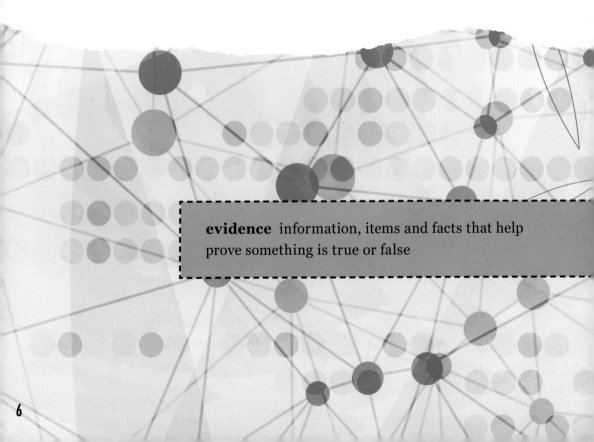

evidence information, items and facts that help prove something is true or false

In the United States, Federal Bureau of Investigation (FBI) agents sometimes help local police solve computer crimes.

CHAPTER 2

Types of computer crimes

Criminals commit more than 1.5 million **cybercrimes** each year. Some criminals want to steal money or get information. **Hackers** may just want to damage computer systems.

criminal someone who commits a crime

cybercrime crime that involves the internet, a computer system or computer technology

hacker person who looks for ways to break into computer systems

❮ Hackers may work together to plan attacks.

FACT
Just one cybercrime can affect computers all over the world.

program series of step-by-step instructions that
tell a computer what to do

Criminals may attach viruses to other **programs** or emails. A virus starts when someone opens the program or email attachment. The virus can then copy itself and damage other computers.

FACT

Sometimes companies hire hackers. The hackers find weaknesses in the companies' computer systems. The companies can then strengthen their systems to prevent attacks.

Some criminals use viruses to shut down computers or to steal **data**. They may ask for money before they will restart the computers or give information back. These viruses are called ransomware.

In May 2017 the ransomware WannaCry spread quickly. It shut down computers at companies in at least 150 countries.

data *information or facts*

Pirates use or copy materials illegally. They often copy music, films and **software**. They may try to sell their illegal copies.

pirate person who uses or copies the work of another without permission

software programs that tell a computer what to do

Some criminals **phish**.
They may send an email with an
attachment. The message tricks
people into opening it. Then a
program allows the criminal to
get information or steal money.

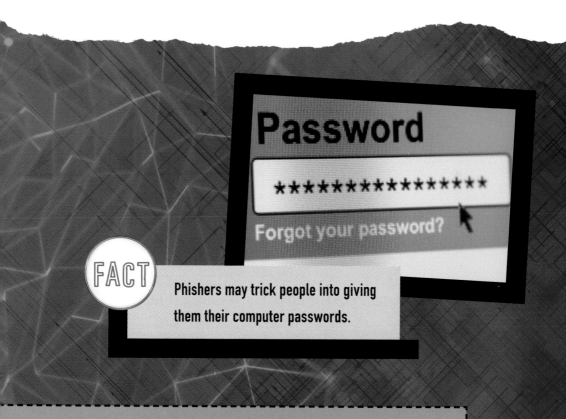

phish pretend to be a trusted person or from a trusted
company to trick victims and commit a cybercrime

CHAPTER 3

Finding and gathering computer evidence

^ a mobile phone found at a crime scene

Police investigators solve computer crimes. They search crime **scenes** for computer evidence. They look for computers, mobile phones and other **digital devices**.

⌃ A crime scene investigator (CSI) checks a computer for clues at a crime scene.

scene place of an event or action

digital involving a computer or other electronics

device piece of equipment that does a particular job

CSI police officer who finds evidence at a crime scene

A CSI wraps a keyboard in a bag to protect evidence.

Police handle devices carefully. They wear gloves. The gloves protect any fingerprints on the items. Fingerprints can help show who has used a device. Police place the devices in bags.

Police often take photographs of devices before moving them. The photos show where the devices were found.

Police take the devices to a crime lab. They search the devices for evidence. They use programs to search computer **hard drives**. Police can even find information that has been deleted.

hard drive device for storing computer data

The hacker group Anonymous is made up of people from all over the world. They claim to hack for causes they support, such as free speech.

⟨ Masked Anonymous members take part in a rally in Manila, Philippines.

An investigator shows a system that allows another hard drive to be read at a lab.

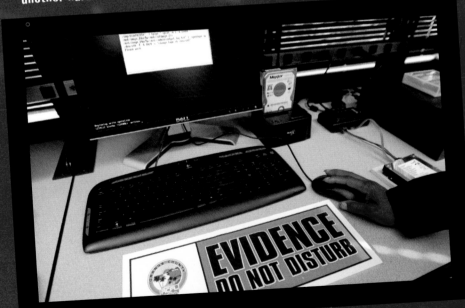

Police may put a tracking device inside a computer keyboard. They return the computer to the **suspect**. The device records what is typed. Police may also put **spyware** on a computer. It tracks websites visited.

suspect someone thought to be responsible for a crime

spyware software that is installed secretly and gathers information about a computer user's internet use and personal data

Police may investigate cyberbullying. This type of bullying takes place through computers, mobile phones and other devices.

An investigator holds a device that can track what is typed on a keyboard.

CHAPTER 4

Computer evidence at work

Police talk about computer evidence in court. They may show what they have found. They may also explain how they found the evidence. This evidence can help to prove that someone is **guilty**.

^ A CSI shows a mobile phone in court
that was collected as evidence.

guilty found to be responsible for a crime

FACT DEF CON is an annual meeting in the United States for hackers. Police and FBI agents also attend.

Computer crimes can be hard to solve. People keep finding new ways to commit these crimes. Police also need to find new ways to find evidence and protect computers.

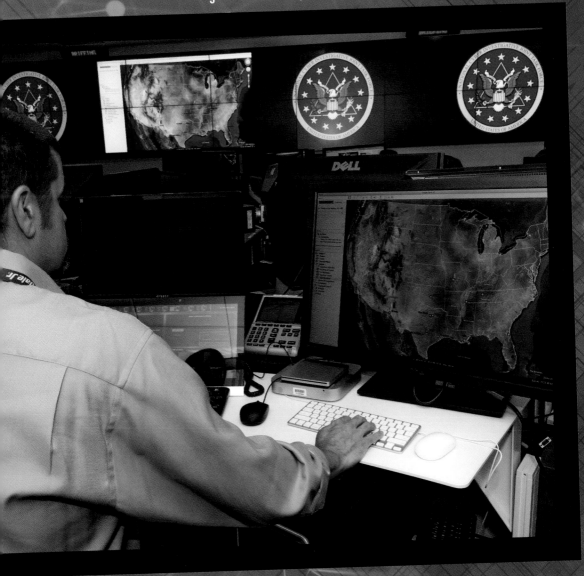

FBI agents and other team members work to protect US government computers from cyber attacks.

GLOSSARY

criminal someone who commits a crime

CSI police officer who finds evidence at crime scenes; in the UK these officers are called Scene of Crime Officers (SOCOs)

cybercrime crime that involves the internet, a computer system or computer technology

data information or facts

device piece of equipment that does a particular job

digital involving a computer or other electronics

evidence information, items and facts that help prove something is true or false; criminal evidence can be used in court cases

guilty found to be responsible for a crime

hacker person who looks for ways to break into computer systems

hard drive device for storing computer data

phish pretend to be a trusted person or from a trusted company to trick victims and commit a cybercrime

pirate person who uses or copies the work of another without permission

program series of step-by-step instructions that tell a computer what to do

scene place of an event or action

software programs that tell a computer what to do

spyware software that is installed secretly and gathers information about a computer user's internet use and personal data

suspect someone thought to be responsible for a crime

track observe or watch the path of something

virus hidden computer program that copies itself and harms computers

FIND OUT MORE

BOOKS

Computer Science and IT: Investigating a Cyber Attack (Anatomy of an Investigation), Anne Rooney (Raintree, 2014)

Crime-Fighting Devices (Science and Technology), Robert Snedden (Raintree, 2012)

Crime Scene Detective, Carey Scott (Dorling Kindersley, 2007)

Forensic Science (DK Eyewitness Books), DK (Dorling Kindersley, 2008)

WEBSITES

www.bbc.com/bitesize/articles/z23q7ty
Learn more about how computer programs work.

www.dkfindout.com/uk/explore/top-internet-tips-to-stay-safe-online
Follow these tips to stay safe online.

COMPREHENSION QUESTIONS

1. What are some ways police protect and record digital evidence they find?

2. Sometimes police return computers to suspects. How can this help the police to solve crimes?

3. What can police look for on suspects' computers and other digital devices?

INDEX

Anonymous 23

court 26
cyberbullying 25
cybercrimes 8, 9

Federal Bureau of Investigation (FBI) 7
fingerprints 20

hackers 8, 11, 23, 28
hard drives 22

labs 22

phishing 17
photos 21
pirates 14
programs 11, 17, 22

ransomware 12

software 14
spyware 24

tracking devices 24

viruses 4, 6, 11, 12

WannaCry 13
websites 24